FORGING
FAITH

Direct Experience
of the Divine

....

**As told through JOHN McKIBBIN
to GATES McKIBBIN**

LIFELINES LIBRARY

For information, contact:

McKibbin Publishing, Inc.
P.O. Box 470091
San Francisco, CA 94147
www.lifelineslibrary.com
www.gatesmckibbin.com

Cover and text design by Kajun Design

Front cover detail from "Judith II (Salome)"
by Gustav Klimt (Cameraphoto/Art Resource)

Author's photo by Christina Schmidhofer

ISBN 1-929799-07-1

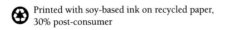 Printed with soy-based ink on recycled paper,
30% post-consumer

*To Saint Paul, whose eloquent wisdom
and definitive insights continue to lead us
to and through our faith*

This book is an affirmation of my own faith—and that of many others. I am grateful for the generosity, mastery and synergy of:

- ♦ **Erin Blackwell**, whose intelligent, insightful editing honored the intention and voice of each message in this volume
- ♦ **Pat Koren** and **Laurie Smith** at Kajun Design, who once again created a glorious book from a mere manuscript
- ♦ **Dick McLeish** at Alonzo Printing, for whom printing my books transcends recycled paper and soy-based ink, and becomes a labor of love
- ♦ **Suzie Daggett**, whose spirited public relations strategy resonates with the purpose and meaning of my writings
- ♦ My steadfast family and friends—and countless others who have shared their stories about what my books have meant to them. Your love sustains me.
- ♦ My collaborators in spirit, who accompany me always on this marvelous journey to the divine

CONTENTS

FAITH

Faith is the palpable belief in the benevolence and loving guidance of the unseen. It arises within your heart. It creates a vortex of the divine within you and emboldens you to reach far beyond your grasp of the physical. Faith alights on your shoulder and whispers words of comfort and hope. It inspires you to trust in the unknowable as if it were right in front of you to be seen, touched and treasured. For faith makes the unseen seen, the distant near, the elusive steadfast.

What measures can you take to bring faith into your life? There is only one, really, and that is to love and forgive without hesitation or condition. When you do that, you are engaging in an act of faith of the highest order. To love another without regard for what is returned to you is to honor the deepest essence of that person. And to honor the deepest essence of another is to have faith in the everlasting love that resides in all that is. For without faith, your love would be conditional and your forgiveness incomplete.

To have faith is to recognize all that is and all that

happens as being a result of the divine. Seeing past the bitterest disappointments, transcending the most painful wounding, healing the most poignant sources of grief: this occurs when you have faith in an expansive wisdom behind it all. For if that faith weren't there, you would remain mired in your tragedies and losses: a world of your own making.

It is a world of your own making because how you respond to what goes on around you is completely within your power to choose and control. Whether you exhibit faith or fear, anger or serenity, greed or generosity is within your own purview. It is not God's actions that make you generous rather than greedy. It is your own actions, which are rooted in your choices, which derive from your faith or lack thereof.

We* will consider the topic of faith in this book of messages from spirit. Far more than you realize, you have the power—every moment of every day—to live in grace. And that grace is a gift of God's love for you in acknowledgement of your faith.

You are blessed with infinite opportunities to grow into your faith. And as you do so, you will experience more joyfully the everlasting power of God's love. But like the most rewarding accomplishments, your faith will not come easily. You will be tested and tested again, each time experiencing the degree to which your faith holds steady or falters. These trials are jewels in the making. They offer you the opportunity to experience yourself returning to your faith in ever more profound ways. They

---

*The *we* that appears throughout this text represents the voice of the spirits who communicated these messages.

present you with a path to God that is devoid of detours —provided that you hold fast to your faith.

We honor you for your desire to live in love and affirm your faith. We understand the challenges that faith presents in your life, for it requires you to see beyond your immediate circumstances, to apprehend the larger principles and patterns embedded in what is occurring, to maintain your goodness without regard to whether others are doing the same. Your faith lights a flame of love in your heart that guides and protects you throughout your journey and enables you to arrive at your destination wiser and with a knapsack full of light and joy and peace.

We love you for taking this book in hand. We will journey together. The path is open to you.

UNSEEN

To have faith is to believe in the unseen as if it were seen. To have faith is to experience the unseen so completely and confidently that, in fact, you can see it.

How can the unseen become seen? Consider all of the ways that you see. You see not just with your eyes, but with your senses. You also see with your mind and your heart. To experience the unseen as seen is to bring it into your consciousness so that, quite literally, you experience it in the same way that you taste, touch, hear and smell physical objects.

To see the unseen is to open your heart to the love that emanates from all that is. To see the unseen power of the Creator is to stand in the light of the holy that resides in all that is. To see the unseen glory of God is to become filled with the peace and joy of the divine.

That is how you see the unseen.

How do you go about cultivating this form of seeing? After all, you cannot get new prescription glasses, or don special optical lenses, or walk into a room with a laser light show in progress. You cannot order reserved seating to see the unseen, nor can you rent a video of it at the shop down the street.

To see the unseen, you must first set aside the often unspoken attitudes that influence how you experience your life as it unfolds before you. You can, on the one hand, define your life in terms of your material world. When you do that, your ability to see is indeed limited to your capacity to apprehend what is in front of you. You see a street full of cars and pedestrians, stoplights and stores. You hear the sounds of the engines combusting fuel, people chattering away, horns honking and doors closing. That is what you see and hear with your eyes and ears. And, in fact, you are seeing and hearing it. We do not question the validity of such sensations.

But we do remind you that there are other ways to see. First, revisit the scene we just described. You can see the same physical activity but from the perspective of spirit. When you engage in that, you discover that what you see is no longer the movement of people and things, but a glowing light emanating from everything. Yes, everything. Metal and concrete, asphalt and glass all glow —albeit not as much as living things. But they have their own light-filled existence, just as you do.

People emanate a powerful magnetic force or aura from their being. Grass, flowers, animals—everything in nature—has a magnificent aura. When you see that glow, you are experiencing a connection with spirit that resides within each aspect of creation. When you sense it without actually seeing it with your eyes, you are seeing the unseen love of God that vibrates within and through every component of your three-dimensional reality.

You can also see with your mind's eye, for your mind

has eyes just as your physical body does. Your mind can create images of an alternative reality not bound by time or space. In meditation, for instance, you can go to a peaceful spot that is just as real to you as if you were physically there. Who is to say that this place your mind's eye sees is any less real than what you can see with your eyes? Indeed, it is no less real. It simply exists in another dimension of reality.

And finally, you can see with your heart. This is the most transcendental form of seeing. It creates within you a vortex of unconditional love actualized by the magnetism of spirit. When you see with your heart, you know— as certainly as you know that this book is in front of you—that at the core of everything is love. You witness apparently loveless acts and recognize both their darkness and their light. You walk into turbulence with a sense of calm at the center of your soul. The calm is evidence of your ability to see the larger dynamics that are occurring, which are all rooted in the play of spirit.

When you see with your heart, you are at peace regardless of your outward circumstances. You feel a quiet joy even as others are grieving. You love where there is hate and forgive amidst anger and attachment. You feel the blessing in whatever is before you, with no need to judge it based on outward circumstances.

When you see with your heart, you see the unseen at work in everything. And you know that that unseen is God—is love.

RECOGNITION

Your faith derives from the recognition of spirit in all that is. Your ability to recognize spirit everywhere fuels your faith, just as your faith enflames your ability to recognize spirit everywhere.

What must you take on faith? You must have faith in the existence of spirit in all of life. What is the requirement of this faith? Your faith requires you to trust that what you can neither document nor prove, actually is.

If you are a rationalist—if you must have foolproof evidence that there is a supreme spirit energy—you will be incapable of experiencing or acting on faith. If your central purpose is to mitigate your material vulnerability at the cost of your spiritual growth, you will believe that faith is irrelevant. If you intend to control every aspect of your life, you will resist even the intimation of faith. For faith necessarily leads you into the realms of the uncontrollable. If you give only when you get and share only when you receive, you will renounce faith. For it requires you to give unconditionally and share without expectation of personal gain.

Where do you begin, then, when you want to be more fully capable of recognizing spirit? You can begin where it makes the most sense—and has the most potential benefit. And that is with yourself.

It is easier for you to experience spirit at work within you because you *are* spirit. Whether or not you recognize it, whether or not you attend to the matters of spirit as you pass through your days, you are spirit. To find the crystal of spirit within your own being is to affirm your most fundamental and enduring quality. To recognize the degree to which spirit serves as a catalyst for every event that occurs in your life is to acknowledge your inviolable connection with all that is. To experience yourself rising above the seductions of selfishness, or the glitter of greed, is to recognize that given the choice, you honor spirit over self-absorption.

Think about the past week. Was there a time when you were given an unexpected gift of love? How did you receive it? Did you experience gratitude for the blessing of this love? Did your heart feel more full and simultaneously less burdened? Did you discover within you a wellspring of peacefulness, clear as a mountain brook? If you were blessed with love in any of its manifestations—whether it was flowing to you, or from you, or in both directions—you were given the gift of spirit.

Recognize that, and you have taken a step toward faith.

Aren't there many who can love but have no faith? Yes, there are, but their love is mired in the material world. It does not soar to the light-filled realms where spirit vibrates with purity and uncompromising splendor. Such love is not available without bonds; it keeps love in the bondage of materialistic objectives.

If you can give and receive love with no other purpose but loving, you have in fact taken a significant step toward faith. For to love is to have faith in the benevolence of God and nature and humanity. To love is to experience empathy with all forms of life, and to recognize the higher reality that is manifest in all.

We urge you to become more conscious of the ways you offer and accept love, honor others and yourself, trust that there is a higher power at work in everything, always and forever. You cannot even begin to understand the depth of your faith if you do not recognize the extent to which love is central to your life. And conversely, you cannot make faith central to your life if you do not love. It all begins with the ability to witness your own pool of vibrant, abundant love within and without. From there you can witness how love leads to faith and attracts more faith-based love to you.

From there, you can proceed toward a more secure, serene way of life.

SECURITY

How can faith enhance your sense of security? Isn't security a materially based aspect of your life? Aren't you more secure when your basic human needs are being met?

Yes, being able to assure your survival in the material world can make you feel more secure. But the ultimate source of your security is faith.

Perhaps you have a good, solid roof over your head, delicious food on the table, money in the bank and enough left over for a splurge every now and then. You are getting your material needs met.

But you may worry about losing it all—or enough of it so that you no longer can count on having the bare necessities. You have enough material resources to feel secure. But in actuality, you are feeling insecure. In fact, sometimes having more resources increases rather than decreases your feeling of insecurity. You become so pre-occupied with maintaining your nest egg that you begin to focus more time and energy on its potential loss than on affirming the blessing of having it in the first place.

That is insecurity.

What if you had faith that as long as you served spirit with your life—as long as your intention is to carry the light-filled flame of love within and express it without—you would be guided to have whatever you needed? If you truly believed that, you would feel secure. There would be no reason to be insecure, would there?

When you start to feel bereft or worried, ask yourself what is causing the erosion of your faith. Is it your attachment to the illusion of security provided by material resources? Is it greed: the desire to accumulate more than you really need, just for the sake of knowing you have it? Is it selfishness: the need to hang on to everything you have so that you can use it to define yourself? Whenever you feel insecure, it is due to a weakening of your faith.

In contrast, take another look at the sources of your sense of security. Are you feeling secure because you have enough for today and the inevitable rainy day? If so, be grateful for such a luxury.

Beyond that, ask yourself this: Are you feeling secure because—regardless of what you have, can count and surround yourself with—you have faith that you will always have enough? And isn't your faith that you will always have enough based on the understanding that, as a servant of God, you are living within the flow of the natural order of things, which provides all of the security that you really need?

Ponder how you are currently getting your needs met. Are you asking for what you need and if so, is it really what you need? Are you working yourself to a frazzle because you believe that you are the only one you can depend on to get your financial needs met? Are you entering willy-nilly into superficial friendships and unstable relationships in order to get your emotional needs met, then emerging from them depleted and disappointed? Are you placing your own needs so far above the welfare of others that you create a spiritual chasm between yourself and your higher consciousness?

Or are you identifying your material, relational and spiritual needs, asking spirit out loud to assist you in meeting those needs, then trusting that you will get your needs met? Granted, they may not be the needs you had in mind. You may not realize until after the fact that they existed at all. You may not be able to anticipate when they are met or in what order, but your needs will be met, nonetheless.

If you are truly committed to walking the path of love and light, if you are genuinely committed to serving spirit with your life, if you desire only to end this life full of love and gratitude for having had the opportunity to grow toward God, you will get your needs met. Every last one of them. From dawn to dusk, year in and year out.

You may be materially wealthy; you may have very little.

You may be quite active in the world; you may lead a solitary existence.

You may display an outward life that others envy; you may live as simply as a monk.

But you will get your needs met. You can have faith in that.

PENETRATE

A magnetic veil has surrounded planet Earth for millennia, keeping people from easily acknowledging the higher dimensions and accessing spirit. They have been unable to penetrate this barrier between the seen reality of the third dimension and the unseen reality of the higher realms. More than ever, people can now transcend the limitations presented by their lives in the physical world. They have the capability of going with their higher consciousness into the realms of the heretofore inaccessible and unknown.

To be able to penetrate the magnetism of the veil around the earth and enter into the wonders of timelessness and spacelessness is a great blessing, indeed. But we are asking you to penetrate something far more difficult and intractable than that. We are asking you to penetrate your own isolating assumptions about what is possible, what is important, what results you are trying to achieve and what really matters in your life.

This is all the more difficult because you persist in giving precedence to the seen over the unseen, the tangible over the intangible. When you do that, you show that you have forgotten your soul's purpose in choosing to be embodied this time. Did your soul make this commitment so that you could go through your days like a mouse in a maze? Did you decide to leave your home in the heavens and return to planet Earth just so that you would have a chance to set aside some karmic baggage? Did your soul plan and prepare for this lifetime so that you could become so caught in the thrall of day-to-day demands that you forgot why you were really here?

In fact, the primary challenge you face is to penetrate the pervasive worldview that what is on this planet and in its solar system is all that is. You may assert that people around the globe believe in a higher wisdom, whatever name they use for it. But most of the time they act as if they didn't. And thus we must question the depth with which they actually hold this belief. If it were truly a guiding principle in their lives, they would factor love and forgiveness and faith into everything they do.

To have faith in the existence of a benevolent Creator is to have a relationship with God that is so dynamic, so compelling, that you cannot not make it central to everything you do and are. To have faith is to live in love as much as—or more than—you live in a country in a continent on planet Earth. To have faith is to penetrate the habit of paying attention only to what is before you materially: your calendar, your job, your bills, your community—and attend also to what is before you in spirit.

When you experience yourself ready and able to embrace the fullness of your spiritual self along with the nature of your everyday existence, you will have penetrated the bonds of your lower consciousness.

COMPELLING

We mentioned in the previous message the goal of having a compelling relationship with the Creator. What does that involve? How can you relate to God without losing your foothold in what most people consider the real world? And beyond that, how can anyone have a relationship with God in the first place, let alone a compelling one?

Faith is essentially a relationship between you and God. You make key decisions based on guidance from spirit, with no other purpose in mind but to serve God. The relationship is so compelling, you trust its basis in love even when you are being bombarded with lovelessness. You understand the necessity of releasing your personal goals in order to contribute to the greater good, even when others around you are attached to their private goals. You recognize the wisdom in the smallest acts and the grandest deeds, even when the tide of opposite forces threatens to sweep your contributions away.

Faith can be the most inexplicably compelling force in your life. We say that it is inexplicably compelling because, contrary to more measurable catalysts for action, faith defies the comfortable parameters of traditional success and failure. You cannot legitimize your faith with compelling arguments or airtight probability analyses. You cannot make a case for your leaps of faith with a linear progression of justifications. You cannot compel others to act on faith based on precedent or prescription. For where faith is concerned, you cannot extrapolate from precedent or prescribe from diagnosis.

Nonetheless, faith can become the most compelling force in your life. Its only rival is unconditional love, which, not surprisingly, is closely aligned with faith. To love unconditionally is to allow yourself to be compelled to give without regard to receiving: to be selfless without a thought of benefit.

Such action cannot be taken in a climate of ambivalence or tentativeness. It is accomplished, rather, because you are compelled, and no other option seems even slightly reasonable to you.

You have a condition that has been labeled *obsessive-compulsive* by Western psychology. Our use of the word *compelling* is closely akin to that—on the surface, at least. Do you have to be obsessed with God to act on faith? Does faith represent, at its most basic, *compulsive* behavior? If faith compels you to act irrationally, how is it different from conditions treated by psychiatrists and psychologists? Who is to say that basing your decisions on faith is any more sane or normal than the case studies documented in medical tomes of mentally ill patients?

There may appear to be only minor distinctions between a compelling faith and psychological imbalance. Neither makes rational sense in modern society. Neither one can be considered normal as defined by your culture. Neither one places the individual in a risk-free position. Quite the contrary, if you define *risk* in the conventional way.

If you are dependent on the acceptance of others, you may avoid acting purely on faith. If you want support for your decisions, you will refrain from doing anything as extreme as taking a leap of faith. If you allow the opinions of others to sway your own, you will not even consider moving forward on the basis of your faith.

But if you trust in the accuracy and authenticity of the guidance you receive from spirit, if you respect your inner knowing to the same degree you trust your reason, if your sense of adventure and willingness to embrace ambiguity are stronger than your need for security and predictability, you may well find that your faith evolves into the most compelling force in your life. And when it does, all other considerations will fall away. You will need nothing more or less than your commitment to serve spirit.

THROUGHOUT

Faith is not something you can practice when it is safe or convenient and discard when you have other priorities. Faith is a hollow commitment unless it pervades all aspects of your life: every moment, every circumstance, every challenge, every commitment.

The imperative of faith is that it be abiding, not transient; steadfast, not ephemeral; patient, not impetuous; steady, not arbitrary.

Faith is not an umbrella you open to protect you during the thunderstorms of your life. Nor is it the straw hat you don on a sunny day to prevent you from overexposure. It is not a pet you play with when you have a few minutes to spare, nor is it the garden you water when you happen to notice that the ground is dry. Faith is neither a luxury when you have plentiful resources, nor an insurance policy you contribute to regularly in case something catastrophic occurs.

Faith must be woven into the warp and woof of your life. Its presence throughout your life—through good times and not so good, crises and celebrations, abundance and scarcity, uncertainty and clarity—is imperative. If you have faith only every now and then, it is not faith at all. It may be a fallback position or a contingency plan, but it is not faith. It may be an anchor during rough seas, but if it is not equally compelling during placid moments, it is not faith. It may be heartfelt when you are filled with gratitude, but if it disappears when you are angry or frustrated, it is not faith. It may be your Rock of Gibraltar at times, but if you lose your footing at the slightest provocation, it is not faith.

We ask you to consider the degree to which faith manifests throughout your life. Notice the moments when it presents itself unbidden and the occasions on which it eludes you despite your efforts to affirm it. Observe when your intention is unabashedly and uncompromisingly to serve spirit and when, instead, your focus is on serving your own best interests.

You can, over time, extend the reach of your faith, make it broader, deeper and more joyful—consciously and with care. Year after year you can grow into your faith until you discover your own unlimited ability to love others and love God. Then the throughout-ness of your faith will be accomplished.

DISAPPOINTMENT

Difficulties and disappointments take the measure of your faith in a way that accomplishments and successes do not. Of course, we wish you success in all of your endeavors to serve spirit, but we also acknowledge the inevitability of some failure. Delights and disappointments go hand-in-hand.

Observe the source of your delight and disappointment. Why do you feel one way on some occasions and another way on others? Most likely you have an impressive list of reasons for feeling different. But try to dig deeper than your immediate criteria for evaluating success and failure.

Your disappointment exists in relation to the expectations that you harbor, whether they are acknowledged or unacknowledged. If you have no conceptions of an optimal—or even acceptable—outcome, you cannot possibly be disappointed.

Disappointment occurs because you have decided in advance which results you want to see from an intervention or action, be it your own action or someone else's.

You think, "If I do this, then this ought to occur as a result." You would be amazed at how many if-then propositions punctuate your consciousness on a daily basis. And each one represents a potential disappointment.

If you entrust the results of your actions to a benevolent higher power, how can the outcome be anything but blessed? How could you possibly determine a more appropriate conclusion? Who could ever have more wisdom and insight than God? How can earthly measures of success be more realistic and relevant than God's? Last but certainly not least, if you surrender to the guiding hand of spirit, how could you ever be disappointed?

Isn't what occurs next, and next, and next, as a result of that surrender, a function of God's will? And isn't God's will the one aspect of your earthly reality that you can trust absolutely? And if your faith in God is so compelling that you are indeed capable of detachment—that you can surrender the outcome of your service to God—then how can any circumstance disappoint you? How could you ever believe that something other than what is, could be more divine than what is immediately in front of you? How could you let your expectations cloud the extraordinary presence of God in everything?

We ask these questions, yet we also recognize that you do become disappointed at times. You are human, after all, and you are not always able to remain detached. Become more cognizant of the occasions when you feel disappointed and the catalyst for those feelings of lack or loss. Turn them over to God. And in their place, affirm your gratitude for everything that is—yes, everything—right now, always and forever.

COURSE

Can you chart a course that will lead to your faith? What is the most effective way to strengthen your faith? How will you know if you are on course or not? And, better still, is there a short course?

There is only one path to enduring faith, and it follows the rhythm of your daily life, year in and year out, lifetime after lifetime. Faith arises not because you have been hit with a thunderbolt revelation of God's grace—although such experiences are possible and can certainly strengthen your faith. But even then, you must find your way through your everyday life, with all of your proclivities and inconsistencies, affirming your faith every step of the way.

You came into your current lifetime with a number of clear intentions regarding your mission: the purpose you want to accomplish, and your lesson: the karmic patterns you want to complete and release. You planned myriad opportunities to do both throughout your lifetime. Whatever serves as a catalyst for you to make spirit-infused choices regarding your mission or lesson is a sign that you are on course. Whatever takes you away from either is an indication that you are off course.

What catalysts keep you on course with your mission? Opportunities to be of service to spirit. What catalysts help you address your karmic lesson? Opportunities to be of service to spirit. And where do these opportunities exist? Everywhere, all the time: in every corner of creation, at every moment.

The fact that you are living this embodiment is evidence enough that you are on course.

This statement may seem cavalier. How does it help you to hear that your mere existence proves that you are on course for affirming and expanding your faith? Now what do you do?

You seize the day. Make the most of each moment. Remain conscious of your immortality as well as your mortality with every breath, every thought. Create in the dirt and dust of the day fertile ground for your faith to blossom. Believe that you can be your most exalted self, whether you are making mashed potatoes or magnificent music. Find your innermost source of serenity, then surround it with your lovelight. Make time to play and laugh, be frivolous and frolic. Do more good deeds than you ever thought you were capable of, then do even more. Do not wait to be acknowledged or honored or even thanked because you have done them. Remember that it is in the doing and the being that you honor spirit.

Your life gives you all you need to remain on course. There is no short course to faith. It cannot be crammed into a weekend intensive program, although it requires total immersion. Faith is inconsistent with perfunctory reassurances, although it can offer you the most reliable reassurance of all: your experience of yourself absolutely and uncompromisingly in service to spirit.

We offer you one more caveat, one more provocation. For what is faith if not provocative as well as providential? Suppose one person is in prison for car theft and another is a selfless single parent working a full-time job and raising two children. Which one is more on course with his or her faith? Using our working definition of faith, that if you are living you are on course, both are equally on course.

How is that possible? Isn't one a more responsible person than the other? Isn't one contributing to society and the other eroding the social fabric? Isn't one living a commendable existence and the other a condemnable one? Does one not honor spirit more than the other?

Recognize the myriad assumptions and value judgments that give rise to these questions. You may equate goodness and altruism with being on course. But in fact, both people have the same freedom to serve spirit, to affirm their faith. God's love permeates prisons as well as devoted households. Your prior choices and immediate life circumstances simply create the context within which you can unite with God or retreat from your faith.

Remember this, the next time you imagine the future implications of your past behaviors. There is no inevitable correlation between the two. You can shift your course to one of caring and spirit any time you want.

BELIEF

Your faith is evidence of your belief in the existence of a pervasive, loving force that is the origin and destination of all life. You yourself derive from this source, and you return to the realms of this source when your soul leaves your body upon your physical death. To have faith is to believe that you have eternal life, which is inextricably linked with the ultimate source of that life.

If you cannot believe in God, you will be incapable of experiencing faith. Unless you can release your need to control all aspects of your life, and instead trust in your ability to surrender to the path of spirit, you will not be living in faith. If you succumb to the habit of evaluating what occurs based on your perception of immediate gain or loss, you will have put your interests ahead of your faith.

Faith requires you to believe not only in God, but also in yourself. Your desire to force your preferred result can be stimulated as much by your insecurities as by your self-confidence. Either way, your ego is confounding your faith. When you strain and pull to manipulate a situation because you feel vulnerable, that is your ego in action. When you strain and pull because you feel you know better than anyone else, that is also your ego in action. Either way, you lose touch with spirit, and thus with your faith.

Your belief that there is a larger reality beyond what you can influence enables you to relax your will. You loosen the bondage of your attachments and desires, discovering instead that your life can be liberated and constantly evolving.

Imagine what it would be like to awake each morning in anticipation of the day—not because you have everything planned in detail, but because you don't. What would it be like to face each day with the abiding belief that it will unfold exactly as it should, in the flow of things, and that you will flow along with it? Think of the value inherent in living your life as a play of consciousness and creativity rather than a plan of attack and victory. The differences are striking.

You cannot release yourself from the stranglehold of your ego's need to govern your every move until you believe that there is a larger reality: an exalted plan and an inspired path for your life. Without that belief, you will create a path and a plan that reflect the limited priorities of your self-serving interests.

Why would you allow your life to be less than it can be, in order to enjoy the temporary reassurance of some instant gratification? Isn't it enough to be blessed with this magnificent lifetime full of potential and promise, and to trust that this potential and promise will become your reality as a result of your faith and good intentions? Can't you let yourself believe that the love that always surrounds you is not shallow, not ordinary, not what you experience in the confines of the physical world? Aren't you willing to trust that the extraordinariness of your existence does not consist solely of the pleasures that you enjoy with your senses, although they are delightful? Can't you believe that the magnificence of your existence derives from your ability to become spirit, to engender spirit, to acknowledge spirit, in unlimited ways and infinite degrees?

You are far more than you usually believe you are. At the roots of your choices and character are your perceptions of your self. These can be unified or fragmented, of flesh alone or spirit in flesh, abundant with grace or lacking therein. Your belief defines who you are, what you are willing to consider to be possible, where you take your life and your life's work, and why you see blessings where others perceive only burdens.

Your belief unburdens your life. It enables you to set aside your frustrations and judgments and desires for more. It creates an interior climate of peace and harmony, whatever your external circumstances. Your belief that you are God made manifest, which derives from your belief in God, is the grandest gift you can give yourself—and the world.

MEANWHILE

While you are living your life, you are also evolving toward God. You may be keeping a full calendar, contributing to your own life and the lives of others. Meanwhile, you are traversing many dimensions of reality as well.

The gift—and the paradox—of being human is that there is a constant "meanwhile" occurring in your life. You are always traveling on multiple journeys in multiple realms. Part of you is living fully on planet Earth, flying around on airplanes, talking long distance on the phone, getting together socially with friends, working at your computer. Another more significant part of you is flying through the realities of timelessness and spacelessness.

You are enjoying a rewarding, fulfilling life here. Meanwhile, you are enjoying a rewarding, fulfilling life there, communing with beings who dwell in the higher realities.

That may seem preposterous to you. You may have no recollection whatsoever of this other existence. The closest you may come is when you remember a dream, although your dreams seem more surreal than real. They hardly qualify as an integral aspect of your reality.

The reality of the higher dimensions includes far more than the dream state, although you do visit those realms in your dreams. It is composed of less dense and more light-filled planes of existence: locales where a significant component of your consciousness finds comfort and meaning. Your body consciousness seeks comfort and meaning on the earthly plane. Meanwhile, your higher consciousness seeks it elsewhere. Both can be satisfied.

The more you allow your spirit free rein, apart from your physical existence, the greater your capacity to embody spirit becomes. And the greater this corollary capacity, the deeper your faith.

Faith is not something you can will into being. You cannot decide that you want to have greater faith in a beneficent higher power, then experience subsequent escalation of your faith.

Instead, faith goes hand-in-hand with your spiritual experience. And that spiritual experience occurs both while you are in your body in the third dimension and when you are out of your body in the higher realms. You treat people with compassion, make integrity-based decisions, find the light in others and strengthen their goodness as well as your own. You also welcome your soul's wisdom: insight it has gained from its peregrinations through multiple realities. Those meanwhiles make your life richer, more complex, and far more meaningful.

LOST

You have to lose yourself to find your faith. And it is this very condition of being lost that most people resist so forcefully. Their resistance is not unfounded. No one is really comfortable amidst the uncertainty of being lost. Even more disconcerting is the directionlessness that typifies the state of being lost. You aren't sure which way is forward or backward, up or down, north or south.

Your faith requires you to plunge yourself into the abyss of unknowing. When you have faith, you no longer need to know for certain how things will turn out, where you will end up or when an answer or resolution will be forthcoming. Faith replaces knowing with unknowing. You shift from having a strategy and a direction to surrendering to the will of God.

Why would you choose such ambiguous circumstances when relative certainty is available? You are a perfectly capable person. You can decide what you want and make it happen. There is nothing wrong with that, is there? Why would you willingly get lost? Isn't that a waste of effort, time and energy?

From the perspective of the physical world you may appear to be lost. But actually, you are plugged into the higher dimensions, where you are anything but lost. In the inner planes you are intensely on mission—and on track. You are not lost at all. You are pointedly, precisely well-situated.

Still, why the focus on being lost? Because you must discard your security-based need to know exactly how your life will unfold. Faith functions only in a context of opportunity for transformation. And transformation requires you to loosen yourself from the moorings of your daily preoccupations.

You cannot truly have faith if you occupy your every waking moment with efforts to manipulate results and force-fit conclusions. You cannot truly have faith if you stick so closely to the strategy you feel will bring you the greatest benefit, you thwart anything that threatens it. And faith threatens it considerably because it requires you to let go—not hang on for dear life.

When you let go of your desire to project your life rationally into the future, and instead trust in the genius of spirit to guide you where you need to be and nudge you to do what is necessary, you appear in the moment to be lost. You could go right or left or straight, depending on your spontaneous inspiration.

But far from being lost, you are allowing yourself to be navigated by the most adept helmsman of all. The course is being charted by your higher consciousness, in collaboration with spirit. There are myriad assurances that you will reach your destination, even if you are unclear about what and where the destination is. You have reason to trust in this navigation. It arises from the founding principles of spirit, which are aligned with all of creation, which is in attunement with God.

Welcome the spirit-based state of being lost, of setting aside your control needs and replacing them with openness and optimism, fluidity and faith. You will find that when you do, your life flows effortlessly. You live comfortably and courageously in the moment. You are often surprised, and the discovery of your spirit, untrammeled by doubt, sustains you through the ambiguity.

You are irrevocably lost and not lost at all. How you see it depends on your consciousness viewpoint.

CONTROL

Your ego is the unenlightened protector of what it perceives to be your best interests. It wishes you no harm. Quite the contrary: its motivations are focused unilaterally on what will secure your current and future survival in the material world. Indeed, your survival in the material world is essential if you are to thrive spiritually. You owe your ego a great deal.

But if you allow your ego to reign supreme, you will unnecessarily contain and constrain your soul's potential to evolve spiritually. You are not here just to survive. You are here to challenge yourself to take leaps of faith, guided by light and love, that defy your ego's stranglehold. You are here to demonstrate such profound and permeating faith, you surprise yourself with the immensity of your courage. Your ego, however, prefers that you reduce or eliminate risk, thus sidestepping any need to act with such courage.

Control plays a variable role in your life, depending on your ego's influence over your perceptions and actions. If you want to maintain the illusion that you can control your own destiny, your ego will be at the forefront of your deliberations and decisions. It will pose questions such as, What do I have to gain from this? What are the risks to me? To what extent can I influence the outcome? Can I pull strings to obtain what I want? What can I get away with, without being discovered?

You can tell that your ego is at work when questions such as these arise.

But when you choose not to give your ego control over your choices, different questions arise. Your musings become less self-involved. You ponder, What am I being guided to do? What would enable me to be of service in the most significant way? How can I embody unwavering light in this situation? What would bring me the greatest gratification and fulfillment?

Your ego's questions target how to control situational dynamics for your own benefit. Your soul's questions derive from the spirit-based reasons for taking one form of action over another. Your ego's questions revolve around the *what* and the *how* of your daily life. Your soul's questions dwell on the *why*.

If you are on track with your contemplation of the why, the rest will fall into place. You will not need to control anything. You can, instead, attend to your flawless inner knowing.

Would you rather spend your days controlling or knowing, containing or expanding, seeing limited certainties or limitless possibilities? The first fork in the road is the one your ego invariably chooses. The second one is preferred by your higher consciousness. One is wedded to the substantive considerations of the material world; the other is guided by spirit. They both have a place in your life. But if you allow your ego to control you, it will gladly and with great enthusiasm smash your spirit.

The more confident you are in your ability to access and integrate the teachings of spirit, the less you will need your ego's ever-present security blanket. Understand that the security your ego provides comes at a great cost to you: the requirement that you turn over some freedom to your ego's control. You can get it back, but not without a struggle. It is far better not to give it away in the first place.

The interplay of your soul's grounding in faith and your ego's attachment to form is both dynamic and perpetual. You will neither be totally consumed by spirit nor totally consumed by flesh. You can, however, be acutely conscious of which one has the upper hand—and why. Ultimately you are the one in control of your destiny. You can best control it by releasing control—and trusting in the light and love of spirit.

FERVENT

Faith requires people to be fervent in their belief. Without an ardent love of God, faith does not survive the trials of daily life. Without a white-hot devotion to selfless service, the seductions of the physical world overtake even the best intentions.

Fervor generates heat, and that heat derives from the fires of unconditional love. Love for God burns. It burns away karmic imprints on your soul. It burns away fears, doubts and resistance. It burns away desires and attachments. It burns away the underbrush of betrayals and setbacks, losses and retributions. This burning is both intense and renewing. Just as forests sprout anew after conflagrations, so is your soul reborn from love's fire.

You cannot believe unreservedly in God if you are incapable of experiencing your love of God—and God's love for you. If the passion is there, so will the faith be. And like all passionate love, faith defies reasonableness. It cannot be justified using logic. It traumatizes the weak-spirited just as it energizes those with the courage to love.

It takes courage to love God—and to act on that love. For to love without condition is to throw yourself open to being tested and tested again. Conditionality threatens the purity of your love of God at every turn. Only if it remains fervent in the context of blatantly compromised love can the passion survive. And when it does, your love grows more intense—and serene.

You are closer to God when your love is tested and then affirmed than at any other time. Then you appreciate how ardent your love really is, if only for a moment. You are filled with love, you radiate light. You look at a beautiful flower or a smiling baby and feel the pulse of spirit coursing between you. You experience oneness with all forms of nature. You are certain that everything is undeniably, without exception, interrelated. All is one. All is essentially one with the One. All is well.

There is no turning back after you have experienced the inimitable passion of God's love. It transforms you at a cellular level so you are physically able to contain a higher love vibration. It transforms you psychologically, so you can surrender in greater degrees to God's love. It transforms you mentally, so you can open intellectually to communication from the divine. It transforms you spiritually, dissolving your body consciousness and enabling you to merge with God.

Feed the flame of your fervent love of God. You may be singed a bit in the process by the material world, but that doesn't mean you should extinguish the flame. Rather, become better acquainted with it. Welcome its comforting heat and glowing light. Be the ardent lover you came here to be.

TREASURE

Consider the nature of a treasure. Priceless jewels, glistening gold, rare fragrances, silken fabrics, timeless documents. Yes, those are all treasures. But the greatest treasure of all—the most magnificent discovery you can make—is the awareness that you love and are loved infinitely, unreservedly, uncompromisingly. God's love is a treasure beyond compare, a bounty of blessings so extraordinary, so marvelous, that it defies explanation.

Love is the gift of the higher self. Love is the jewel that shines brighter than the grandest diadem. Love is the crown of light above your head and the warm resonance within your heart. No other treasure on heaven or earth compares with that of God's love. No other blessing is more resplendent than that of love, given and received freely and unhesitatingly.

Why is it, then, that so much human endeavor has been motivated by the discovery, acquisition and confiscation of the other sort of treasure? Consider the civilizations that have been obliterated, the histories that have been lost to humankind, in the pursuit of treasures. How could greed and gold wreak such havoc? Why is material treasure accorded a value so out of proportion with God's treasure?

It is the human condition to struggle with the temptations of the physical world. Material objects are tangible. They can be objects of great beauty, rivaling even the extraordinary resplendence of nature. They also can be possessed and protected, guarded and hoarded. A sunset cannot be owned, nor the exalted qualities of the heavens.

The collective consciousness of humankind is fraught with the suffering and sacrifice that have occurred at the hands of treasure hunters, be they soldiers or sycophants. You carry within your cellular memory every division of the spoils of battle, every desecration of sacred space, every acquisition through deceit and desperation. You also carry within your cellular memory every act of generosity and selflessness, forgiveness and unconditional love. Unfortunately, the former outweigh the latter.

Consider what you treasure. Anything that you spend time, energy and resources doing, attaining, keeping or maintaining, qualifies as a treasure in your life. When you inventory what you treasure based on these parameters, you may well be shocked. Are you placing more emphasis on material than spiritual treasure? If so, it is never too late to shift the balance. Give away what you no longer need. Simplify your life. Surround yourself with what you truly love—not everything you think you should have. Then honor who and what remains in your life for the treasures that they are—and see all else as a superfluous distraction.

You may not be a conquistador sailing home with a

ship's hold laden with gold. You may not be a wealthy industrialist with a mansion full of Impressionist art. You may not be an entrepreneur piling up properties, just like Boardwalk and Park Place on the Monopoly board. But you still may treasure things over wisdom, objects over insights and possessions over love. If that is the case, find the wherewithal within yourself to shift this pattern. You will confirm your faith in the process. You will not regret it. Untold treasures await your discovery.

SERENITY

With all of this talk of affirming faith despite reluctance and real world ramifications, you may be wondering why anyone would choose such a course. Odds are it won't be worth the effort, given your inevitable human frailties. Are the ongoing trials and need for vigilance anything more than a futile drain on your time and energy?

No doubt, faith requires a huge commitment of your whole self. What is at the other end of it all?

Peace of mind, that's what, and a serenity that redefines for you the meaning of the word. Faith helps you remain serene not just when you are doing well and have enough, but also when you are facing obstacles and scarce support. Whatever your outward circumstances, your peacefulness within prevails.

What is the source of this serenity? It is the profound awareness that you are loved and guided and cared for by spirit. It is the insight that the external conditions surrounding you have little or no connection with your inner truth. It is the abiding faith that if you dedicate your life to the service of spirit and stay the course despite the traumas and troubles that confront you, yours will be a life well lived.

Serenity derives from your ability to discard the implied connection between the measurable and the intangible. The former is neither representative of, nor a substitute for, the latter. In fact, one bears little relationship to the other.

If you look outside yourself for sources of serenity, you realize how ephemeral they are. When things are going your way, you are serene. When they are not, you are full of anguish. The arbitrary apportioning of gains and losses, be they real estate or relationships, creates disequilibrium. You forfeit your serenity, which can be enduring, for your security, which can never be. You lose a great deal in the bargain and benefit little, if at all.

How do you cultivate this serenity? What must you sacrifice for it? And in the end, what assurances do you have that you ever will experience oneness with the divine even once, let alone on a regular basis?

It is ironic that if you seek serenity in the same way you pursue a purpose, it will elude you. Why? Because you will be constantly monitoring your progress, evaluating your effectiveness, trying harder to be serene. But you cannot experience serenity by working at it.

Serenity arrives in your life unbidden, sometimes during the greatest tribulations you will ever experience. It graces your being not because you have set a goal of achieving serenity, then worked diligently to accomplish it. Rather, serenity is a blessing from spirit that descends into your consciousness because you exhibit faith despite the challenges. You affirm your faith regardless of setbacks and misfortune. The more extreme the tests of your faith—and the more one-pointed your faith as you experience these trials—the more penetrating your serenity.

These tests are inevitable. They are inherent in the potent interplay of consciousness and human form on planet Earth. The basis of this interplay is your ability to embody spirit. You always have the option of choosing faith over fear and love over hate. Nothing is getting in your way except your own inability to recognize and embrace the true nature of who you are.

You came into this lifetime to love in the face of its opposite and give generously of yourself despite others' selfishness and avarice. You committed to taking embodiment again, not so that you could sail through life with no responsibilities, but so that you could embrace the breathtaking responsibility of shifting the magnetics of the planet to love and light. That requires you to rise to the occasion and adopt the perspective of the divine in everything that you think, believe, do and say. And, even more importantly, you must do that regardless of what comes back to you—what you have or receive, what people assume or declare about you.

And when you do that, you discover your extraordinary capacity to be a vehicle for light and a medium for spirit. That capacity is there, ready to be accessed and strengthened and appreciated. And inside that capacity is a sea of serenity, one in which you can calm the cacophony of the day and soothe the soreness from your arduous journey. This sea of serenity envelopes you with its comforting fluidity and reassuring support. It encompasses your consciousness and inspires your most marvelous creativity.

Become it. You wear it well.

ECSTASY

Divine rapture commemorates your deepening, resilient faith. These moments of ecstasy take you far beyond your physical body and immediate surroundings into a state of bliss. In this state you experience the unity of all creation. You are at one with the divine and everything that has arisen from God. This interconnectedness is overwhelming. No other perspective on reality is relevant. Only oneness is real. The rest is illusion.

Throughout the millennia people have experienced such ecstatic states. Saints have left their physical bodies to such an extent that they were presumed dead. But actually, a significant portion of their consciousness was exploring the higher realms. They experienced the same vibrational reality that all souls return to after the body dies.

Ecstasy or rapture involves absolute surrender to the realities beyond the material world. It requires you to leave your body behind to a far greater extent than you normally do when you are sleeping or meditating. You must detach from your body as the primary defining factor in your life and greet a considerably more powerful and pervasive spiritual existence.

This necessitates far more letting go than you may realize at first. You are almost inextricably wedded to your body as a source of grounding and architecture for your being. To step away from that is to enter an unfamiliar world, where you are no longer the person you are accustomed to being. Your individualized self merges into a oneness unified with all of creation. You simply cannot remain a physically and psychologically disconnected individual if you are to merge with the One.

These experiences of rapture are unequivocally transformative. It is impossible to experience the full reality of timeless, spaceless existence and return to this body in this lifetime with the same assumptions you held before. You are incapable of acting in ways that serve only your own interests. You understand implicitly the impact that your judgments, emotions and attitudes have on everyone and everything else. You can no longer hide behind the protection of an "Oh well, it doesn't matter anyway" approach to life. On the contrary, you are acutely aware that everything matters, everywhere, always.

Rapture results in a sharpening of your sense of the divine within you, and of your concomitant responsibility to honor the divine with your wholeness. Rather than disengaging from the world, you reengage. But your reengagement is from a radically altered mindset and heart place. You are engaged in the world not as one person among many, but as someone who is at one with all. This at-oneness remains in the forefront of your altered consciousness.

Selflessness is no longer in conflict with the preservation of your self because you have merged with the all. Thus selflessness becomes the most exalted expression of your self. You no longer struggle to be detached, since you realize that material outcomes represent only a tiny portion of reality. You no longer sense the futility of your efforts to make a difference in the world, since your ability to embody spirit is both the means and the end of your existence.

Ecstasy is at once a consecration and a catalyst. It is a consecration in that it opens the portal to God. It enables your higher consciousness to experience clearly and concretely the realities of the divine. It is a catalyst because once you have experienced this exalted way of being, you can never return to your former state. You are thrust into an expanded reality with equally expanded obligations. You must live in the world, but in a way that honors your inherent oneness with all.

The wonderment of the rapture remains, however, even if you experience it only once and never again. It is a lighthouse for your soul, pointing the way during your peregrinations and lighting the path back home. The light is never extinguished, for the love that you bring back with you from this ecstasy is fully integrated into your being. You are love. You are light. You are the divine first and foremost.

KNOWING

You can, with intention, deepen your ability to discern the messages and essential truths of spirit. That, in turn, enhances and expands your faith. Both intention and faith are sources of vitality.

Your ability to distinguish visions and voices of spirit from those of the physical world is central to your role as a servant of spirit. You have remarkable intellectual and perceptual capabilities. But these capacities confound your discernment because they seem so appropriate and valuable. It is easy to be persuaded that an idea deriving from your rational mind is actually spirit-based. It is equally easy to be induced to believe that an insight you received from spirit originated in your own mind.

One of the ways you can grow and ground your faith is to develop your ability to differentiate what you know from an intellectual perspective from what you know from a spiritual perspective. As you can imagine, the two are as different as clay and crystal.

Your mind is an extraordinary storehouse and processor of knowledge. You know that the Spanish word for love is *amor* and that Iceland is located in the Northern Hemisphere and that curry consists of spices. You also know with your senses, which send stimuli to your mind for interpretation. You know that feather down is soft, knives are sharp and your digital clock indicates that it is 7:44 p.m.

That is a legitimate, provable form of knowing. It makes your life far more convenient, productive and enjoyable than it would be without your brain and body's abilities to know so much.

But that isn't the only form of knowing available to you. You also have the capacity of discernment: the knowing that derives from spirit. Your higher consciousness is involved in discernment just as your mind is involved in your intellectual knowing.

One way to tell the difference between intellectual knowing and discernment-based knowing is to perceive the vehicle by which the information arrives. If an idea results from a lengthy or even abbreviated thought process, it most likely has its roots in your intellect. But if it arrives spontaneously and holistically, it could well be a message from spirit. With the former you engage your intellect; with the latter you must disengage your intellect.

There is another way to recognize the validity of your discernment. And that is when you just know that what you are feeling, sensing, hearing or envisioning is true. Your inner capacity to sense the spirit vibration and love embedded in the insight can be honed with great precision. Over time you will grow to trust it more and recognize its authenticity. Then you have an invaluable ally: your relationship and connection with spirit through discernment.

You need never stop learning or challenging yourself intellectually. You also need never feel abandoned by spirit. When you remain open to the love vibration that is within and around you, when you trust the guidance you are receiving even if it runs contrary to what seems reasonable, when you call upon spirit for assistance and get the response you need in a flash of insight or a synchronistic event, you are utilizing your full capacity as a spirited human being. When you act on your discernment, you are respecting and affirming your faith.

FRAGILE

We have given this book the title of *Forging Faith* after considerable deliberation. Indeed, you must forge your faith. Like well-tempered steel, it will emerge from the fires molten and red hot. What you do with it at that point bears noting. For molten steel can be hardened into a block or girder as easily as it can be made into a saber or stiletto. Your shaping of your faith determines the role it plays in your life.

Forging is necessary because of the inherently fragile nature of faith. It is not like an inoculation against fear or hatred. Nor is it a negotiated treaty between your higher and lower consciousness, with assurances of mutual responsibility and sanctions built-in, just in case they are not honored.

Faith forms the structure of your life as you address each moment of each day. You may be feeling quite faith-full, only to experience an unanticipated assault on your faith. The resulting disequilibrium causes you to distance yourself from spirit. Darkness is well acquainted with the fragility of your faith. It can target quite precisely the one area of your life that is most vulnerable to doubt, then feed it relentlessly.

Like everything else in life, your faith grows stronger only when it is challenged and you choose to follow faith-based principles. There is no room to maneuver around these challenges or take a half-hearted approach to affirming your faith. Your intention to hold fast to your faith reduces its fragility and forges a strong, dependable foundation for your life.

Why is your faith so fragile? Can't God intervene to make it stronger? And if it is so elusive, isn't it futile to try to strengthen your faith?

To equate fragility with futility is to misperceive the essence of faith. Faith derives from your ability to trust in the unknowable. That is no small task, given your propensity to define reality in terms of the materially provable or intellectually knowable.

You must continue to follow the path of faith no matter what occurs in your life. Optimally, what manifests immediately in front of you will have no bearing on the stability of your faith. And yet it does. The most predictable assaults on your faith stem from the circumstances of your daily existence. Spirit cannot and will not intervene to make life easier or to mitigate the voices of insecurity and fear that you often hear.

So your faith remains fragile. You will be quite taken aback at the ease with which it can be shaken to the core. We see the potential for constancy even though we frequently observe its inconstancy. Unlike an ordinary emotion, your faith derives from the deepest essence of your being. And within that essence is either infinite love or shallow desire, clarity of purpose or confused anxiety.

You forge faith every time you confront the aspects of your spiritual essence that make you less than whole, that take you away from your most steadfast source and lead you into the lair of limitation. You alone have the capacity to recognize your inherent grace and goodness. You alone have the capacity to identify and mitigate the influences that make your faith so fragile.

There is a paradox here, of course. The very fragility of your faith provides the necessary stimulus for you to forge your faith. Without the discrepancies between what you say you believe and how you actually address each situation you encounter, you would be unable to temper the steel of your spirit. The heat of your love of God is never so intense as when it is threatened, then affirmed, then acted upon. Every time you choose faith over fear, you transform fragility into tensile strength.

Take care of your internal well-being along with your external circumstances. Only then can you forge faith from your fragile frailties.

ENLIGHTENMENT

We often refer to enlightenment as if it were as easily comprehensible as starting a car or plugging in a lamp. And in a way, enlightenment is no more complicated than that.

This assertion may startle you. We have sent down volumes of messages that tell of enlightenment. We have approached the subject from every conceivable angle, warning you of the detours that must be met and the distance that must be traveled. How can we then make light of enlightenment?

No doubt, if you could turn enlightenment on like a 100-watt bulb, you would. And you can, but not with the force of your will, professional expertise or stature in the community. All it takes is an unwavering focus on your love of God and commitment to be of service.

"Oh, is that all?" you say. "Just do the most difficult thing I can imagine, and then enlightenment will be mine. That's a little harder than starting my car."

That is a perfect example of how your doubts limit your potential. We assert that enlightenment is available to you, and you immediately question the veracity of the declaration. We suggest that you can achieve enlightenment as easily as flipping a switch in your soul, and you refuse to believe that such a switch could possibly exist. And even if it does for some people, you assume that yours was not correctly installed. We offer an image of your being an enlightened servant of God, and you take off in the other direction as quickly as your lower body consciousness can get you going.

Why is that? Why can you believe almost anything about yourself more easily than the assertion that enlightenment is immediately available to you?

You have been bombarded by reminders of your fall from grace so many times, you find it almost impossible to imagine that such grace could ever again be a central aspect of your life. And what reminds you so incessantly of that fall? Your fears and frustrations, hypocrisies and hurts, memories and mornings after. You know yourself quite well, and that self with whom you have become so intimately acquainted is not enlightened. If that is true, then how can enlightenment be possible, or even likely?

You already are spirit, which resides in the flesh. Therefore, a significant aspect of your being contains the seed crystal of love and light. You are love and light to some degree, even when you are feeling or acting loveless and dark. If you are love and light to some extent, then you must be love and light wholly. How else can light exist in your being?

Spirit, which manifests as light and love, is inherent in all creation. And that spirit is so pervasive, dominant and omnipresent that in the face of it, nothing else can exist. Where there is light there can be nothing but light.

You are the emanation of the God-force. Without the spark of spirit you have no life. But you do have life, and it continues infinitely. Your life is eternal, as is the light of spirit that resides within you. That light will never be extinguished. It may be diminished; it may flicker and falter; it may be temporarily displaced by opposing forces. But your light will always be with you, whether your soul is in a denser physical mass called a body, or liberated in a more rarefied existence in the higher realms.

You have life; therefore, you are light. If you are light, then you are en-light-ened. Yes, you are already enlightened.

Imagine the implications for a moment. If you are already enlightened, then you can cease struggling with the darkness. You can surrender your will to faith in God, unreservedly and unhesitatingly. If you are already enlightened, you have the option of seeing your material reality for exactly what it is: a stage setting on which the karma of the human species is being played out. If you are already enlightened, you can transcend that karma by recognizing your own role in it, then transforming it to ecstatic spirit and oneness.

Karma divides; spirit unites. Darkness overshadows; light illuminates. Doubt destroys; love creates.

You have the option of following two vastly different life trajectories. One denies your intrinsic union with God and establishes a corporeal paradigm for your being. The other acknowledges your enlightenment and establishes the veracity of your higher consciousness, which lives in light, which is your being unqualified and undiluted.

Do not think about your own enlightenment, allow

yourself to be it. You will never fully believe in your enlightenment until you experience it as the essential, singularly defining factor of your self. It is time for you to believe that such a thing is possible.

FORGIVENESS

To have faith is to be willing to be forgiven. God forgives all, immediately and comprehensively. There is nothing you can do—*nothing*—that is not forgiven.

But you do not perceive yourself as worthy of such forgiveness. How can you be worthy, when the choices you make betray your faith in spirit? Deep down, as well as right on the surface, you do not feel that you deserve to be forgiven. And thus you hang onto your sins and debilities as if they were badges of honor to be shown off at every opportunity.

This inability to allow yourself to be forgiven thwarts your ability to forgive not only yourself but others as well. If you assume you are unworthy of forgiveness, you are unlikely to find others worthy either. And you most certainly will be unable to forgive yourself. So you perpetuate the cycle of guilt, which reinforces your unworthiness, which distances you from the spirit within, which causes you to believe that you are unenlightened.

You see, then, how much begins and ends with forgiveness.

What is underneath this inability to forgive? It is the incapacity to love unconditionally. The moment you place conditions on your love, you establish criteria by which to evaluate what can and cannot be forgiven. If you can love only under certain circumstances, then you can forgive only under similar circumstances. The more conditional your love, the greater your inability to forgive. So the cycle of unavailable love and inaccessible forgiveness perpetuates itself.

Let us return to the simple yet almost inconceivable assertion that whatever you do—whoever you are—God sees, loves and forgives you. Can you for even a moment let yourself feel seen, loved and forgiven? If so, what happens?

Initially, you feel immensely unburdened. The weight of guilt and unworthiness vanishes from your psyche. You feel lighter, more playful, more able to imagine an unfettered existence.

Then you begin to realize the degree to which your self-assessments have held you back. You see with new eyes the many occasions on which you chose the less love-based approach because of your inability to love yourself. You understand the bittersweet moments when you could have breathed from the fullness of your being and instead retreated into your unworthiness.

When you forgive, you honor God—and your most marvelous spiritual beingness—with the gift of your compassion, caring and commitment to loving. When you open yourself to being forgiven, you set yourself on a course of renewal and rebirth, everlastingly.

FORGIVEN

When you forgive another, you release all expectations of receiving what you perceive to be due you. You may expect an apology, the payment of a debt, the honoring of an agreement or compensation for a transgression.

When you forgive, you let go of your attachment to the desire for a specific response or behavior from another. You cleanse from your physical, psychological and spiritual being the anger, judgment making and victimization that have been festering inside.

Forgiveness shifts the vibratory patterns of the cells within your physical body. This enables you to release the memory of the trespass that is being held within your physical being as you also emancipate yourself psychologically and spiritually. Blaming and conditionality, which keep you from being able to forgive, create irritations that influence your biochemistry. This in turn affects everything from your immune system to your sense of well-being. You are healthier in all ways when you can forgive.

Pious self-righteousness often accompanies the

inability to forgive. You convince yourself that you have only minimal responsibility for the situation—that the disequilibrium that exists is a function of the other person's irresponsibility, duplicity or hypocrisy. You embroil yourself in an energy vortex of judgmentalism, negative emotions and hostile behavior. And that does not serve you.

As long as you hang onto the idea that someone owes you something, you disempower yourself. The closure and healing you desire are subject to the choices of another, not you. When you cannot forgive, you allow someone else's attitudes and actions to hold you back. When you cannot forgive, you intensify the connection you have with the other, which is rooted in a fallen aspect of your relationship. You are restricted by bondage of your own making, which weakens your faith in yourself and others. You must forgive in order to release yourself as well as the other person.

You can forgive and still make every effort to recover what is due you. The difference is that after you have forgiven the apparent transgression, your further communication about it derives from a place of detachment rather than attachment. You act for the purpose of maintaining the integrity of the situation. You provide an opportunity for the other to act with equal honor and integrity. If they do, you both benefit. If they don't, you are not held back by the other's choices.

Make a list of everything you are ready to forgive. Affirm your forgiveness by writing it or saying it out loud. Then release unconditionally the metaphysical obligation that has connected you with all of the people you have not forgiven until now.

Give yourself the gift of forgiveness. You will be more joyful and less ready to see the worst instead of the best in yourself and others. Your faith will be less vulnerable to the vagaries of your personal associations and material transactions.

Forgiveness unburdens your soul. It is an act of love—a potent way to honor spirit. Forgive, and you take another step toward God. Forgive all, including your own weaknesses and blunders, and you live in perpetual grace.

COMPASSION

Compassion is the ability to feel with another, to experience oneness to the point of merging with her or his inner being. You do not become the other; rather, you create a union that honors your separateness and your shared divinity.

The basis for compassion is the open-hearted, non-judgmental ability to see God in another being. You cannot be truly compassionate if you are incapable of recognizing and resonating with the spirit of another. That spirit carries within it all current realities and distant memories of that individual's existence. To be compassionate is to create an effortless flow of acceptance and insight between yourself and another.

Do not take on the pain, patterns or priorities of the other, however. You must not forfeit your own boundaries in order to relate more compassionately with him or her. Instead, allow yourself to flow in and out of your inner experiences together.

The willingness to risk compassion arises from your heart-wrenching awareness that separateness is a misperception. We are all one with God and thus are one with each other. The spirit that is within you and all of creation unites you with all creation.

When you begin to integrate this almost unfathomable notion, you discover that your compassion has blossomed like a flower in the spring sunshine. The previous decisions that kept you safely apart from others dissolve in the realization that there are no divisions between you.

Compassion is not the sort of thing you bring into your life or your relationships with a preordained sense of the possible. It surprises you with its subtlety and significance. Rather than consciously deciding to be compassionate, you simply notice yourself behaving that way. You awaken your sleeping consciousness with the glimmer of your ego's dissolution into unconditional nonjudging.

It is at once straightforward and a bit stupefying. If you can be compassionate, then what else is possible? Have you understated your own spiritual capacity? And can your compassion extend beyond your idiosyncratic relationships with people you know? Can you feel compassion toward strangers, foes, flagrantly misguided souls?

Compassion enables you to feel with another. It is a blessing for the giver and the recipient. Acknowledge what your compassion communicates about you: your open-heartedness, egolessness and most of all, your spirited humanity.

WILL

You are accustomed to succeeding in great measure by the force of your will. That strategy works well in the material world. Often the person with the strongest will wins, and thus enjoys the fruits of victory. Your language acknowledges the process: *being strong-willed, a test of wills, to will something into being.* People with strong wills are revered for their ability to have their way regardless of influential forces to the contrary. That is considered a healthy, and perhaps even venerable, quality.

Where does faith fit in here? For the most part, it doesn't. If you intend to achieve what you deem most propitious by force of will, you will be incapable of surrendering to the degree required by faith.

Faith has one mantra related to will: *Thy will be done. Thy* will—not *mine*—be done. Thy will: not what *I* perceive to be best for *me* or anyone else. Thy will: not what the majority says they want.

Thy will be done. This is the essence of releasing control over the outcome of your actions. This is the most fundamental statement of faith. It is also an affirmation of your ability to release the need to force one conclusion over another.

The will of God—not your own—is the ground on which you affirm your faith. The will of God—not the result you would prefer—is what you want to see achieved. The will of God—not your innermost desire—is what you ask God to deliver.

When you say, "Thy will be done," you quite literally are requesting and affirming that God's will be dominant, whatever the situation. You may pray for the revitalized health of a friend or the success of a business venture, but when you end with the avowal, "Thy will be done," you are surrendering the outcome to the will of God.

When you surrender to God's will, you also give over the conclusion to a non-negotiating power. You attest that such a power is so omniscient, it far transcends whatever feeble hold you may be trying to maintain over your existence. When you surrender with the words, "Thy will be done," you offer your faith with nothing in your heart but your trust in God and your love of God.

When you offer your own will as recompense to God, you strengthen your faith. You also disengage from the need to control what happens next, then next, then next.

That is surrender. It is at the heart of the prayer, "Thy will be done."

Consider the words that follow this phrase in The Lord's Prayer:

Thy will be done

On earth

As it is in heaven

There is immense wisdom in that prayer. For it

requests that God's will be as dominant—and apparent—on the physical plane as it is in the higher realities.

On earth

As it is in heaven

When you turn your will over to God, you ask not just that a higher power pass the wisest and most compassionate judgment, but that the transcendent realities of the heavenly realms exist in this less than transcendent, earthly plane. You ask with all your heart that God bless the situation with nonjudgmental understanding, unconditional peace and irrevocable wisdom.

If you are asking God to intervene to create a reality here that is commensurate with what is there, then you are suggesting that the material world can be influenced by timelessness and spacelessness. And if you believe that, then you understand that the relevance of a higher reality can be considerably strengthened by your willingness both to surrender to it and to accept whatever it yields without question, regret or redefinition.

"On earth as it is in heaven." What more marvelous prayer exists than that? It causes you to look beyond what you see, know and value right in front of you. It gives you the power of detachment, which releases you from the need to manipulate things in your favor and replaces that with the awesome capability and consequence of your faith.

When you have faith that the will of God as it exists in heaven can also manifest on earth, you witness the inexorable flow of the human condition in and out of embodiment. You recognize that the soul is at once unenlightened in its earthly quests and consummately enlightened on its spiritual path. It is both a beacon and barrier, a cause and contradiction. The soul is simultaneously grace and grit.

Whenever you are tempted to believe that you know what is best, stop to consider what you don't know. Your own understanding of the dynamics influencing any one situation is starkly limited, compared to what is actually occurring. You cannot perceive the totality of the process with your rational mind. Only when you release the need to know—and control—and begin to see with your inner eyes can you discover that, in fact, God's will has been in effect all along. It always has and ever will be.

Surrender to it. Then and only then can you find the fullness of grace that accompanies such revelations.

PRAYER

At its most basic and thus most powerful, prayer is an opportunity for you to create a direct link with spirit. That is possible, wholly and completely. What you do with that link, once you have established it, is the key to prayer.

Many people make demands or requests of God. They appeal for the manifestation of specific results. Relieve the sadness I feel, find me a good job, help me meet someone to marry. These requests represent a central concern in your life. But from the perspective of spirit, they may be only at the periphery of what you came into this lifetime to become and to accomplish.

Why squander a direct connection with God on something tangible that you want to have or have happen? God's love is so potent, it can manifest anything for you. It can help you experience the pervasive unity of all creation. It can enable you to walk among the most pitiful strangers and feel closer to them than you do to your own family and friends. It can enable you to give so generously of yourself and your resources that all you know when it is over is that you have served God.

When you pray, be conscious of your underlying intentions. If you are trying to get something from God—to beg so persuasively that your wishes be granted—then you are out of touch with the purpose of prayer. If, instead, you pray for no reason other than to forge a strong bond with God—if you ask for nothing but to be blessed with further insight and inspiration in order to be of even greater service—then that bond will be enduring indeed.

Of course, God hears all entreaties, egotistic and humble alike. Any attempt to come into contact with God's love is welcomed. But when you pray with no intention other than to fill your heart with more exquisite light and more expansive love, you dwell in the realms of the heavenly power of God. And those realms consist of limitless love, unfettered grace, ineffable peace.

That is the purpose of prayer. Pray to honor God, and your heart will be still. There will be no more striving.

Do it, and you will immerse yourself in the peaceful pool of love, which is the ever-present God, God's everlasting love, God's gift to you.

Do it, and you bless yourself with the omnipotent yet serene mercy of the divine.

Do it, and your supplications fall away. In their stead you find humility born of the wondrous nature of God's benevolence, which needs no proof, defense, justification or enhancements.

Do it, and you need nothing else but prayer itself, which is whole and beautiful, gracious and good in and of itself.

POSSIBILITIES

Anything is possible. You can evolve so rapidly and compellingly toward spirit in this lifetime that no further embodiments are necessary to complete your karma. You can also fall from grace to such an extent that you obliterate the progress you have made—and perhaps regress to an unevolved point further behind than you have ever been.

There is ample evidence that people are capable of devolution. There is also ample evidence of the opposite. If you are going to focus on possibilities, why not attend to the more satisfying, spiritually oriented ones?

You create reality from possibility by giving it your attention, emotion, talent, expertise or resources. Whatever you think about or are emotionally tied to—whatever you invest your time and energy in influencing—has a much higher likelihood of manifesting.

You may truly believe in the potential of all people to embody spirit fully. But if you worry or fuel assumptions to the contrary, you will actually help create the opposite result. What you choose to imbue yourself with moment to moment matters more than what you believe you believe. The measure of your beliefs is not what you purport to believe, but what your actions express.

What if you could believe that wondrous things are always possible—and then acted on that belief as you went about your days? You would find spontaneous joy and unanticipated opportunity at every turn. You would welcome events that challenge you to excel beyond your previous limits and test your faith in the process. You would have no fear to overcome because your attention would be unilaterally focused on what is possible—not what seems impossible. Thus you would create a spirit-based reality from possibility.

Assess what you currently consider impossible. It may be something as apparently insignificant as your ability to keep house plants alive. It may be as huge as your completion of a graduate degree. Whatever you think is impossible will most likely remain so.

But what if you took the list of impossibilities and turned them into their opposite? What if you came to understand not only that you have infinite potential, but that you have unlimited support in achieving that potential? The combination of your intentions, your belief in the possible and the support you receive along the way gives birth to a new reality. You created it yourself, with a little help from spirit. You transformed a possibility into a reality.

Consider your spoken assumptions and unspoken attitudes. Everything from your social milieu to your secular preferences can hold sway over your perceptions. Explore how the perspectives that surround you influence your choices. You may be surprised at the extent to which you hesitate or even halt, refuse or even resist because the stronger pull lies on the side of what appears impossible or unlikely.

Of course, simply saying that something is possible makes it neither a given nor necessarily attainable. Most accomplishments require patience and perseverance, short-term energy and long-term enthusiasm. To transform a possibility into a reality can be a remarkable achievement. But remember that your beliefs and assumptions influence the result as much as your hard work.

When the unconscious becomes conscious—and when the conscious is guided, framed and mentored by higher consciousness—the reality that unfolds from possibility manifests the work of spirit combined with your own.

TEMPTATION

Many issues and events will tempt you away from your faith. The more obvious, recognizable ones will be difficult enough to address as you find your way through your days. But other, more surreptitious temptations may have even more impact because of their ability to tempt you within the context of your unknowingness.

Discernment never plays a more central role than when you are tempted away from spirit. A temptation is by its very nature, something that initially appears to be desirable in relation to your current circumstances. You are tempted because you prefer what is being offered.

But temptation carries with it another dynamic. You must give up something in order to indulge the temptation. For example, you may be tempted to order a rich dessert after a special dinner in a lovely restaurant. You must weigh your enjoyment of the dessert, which is likely to be considerable, with what you might need to give up (an equal number of calories) or do more of (exercise) later.

That is a simple illustration. The point is not whether

you should order the dessert. And we certainly do not mean to imply that yielding to temptation is unspiritual. But if you do it a lot—if you eat many, many rich desserts and do nothing to compensate for them—you will pay a price that may well not be worth the enjoyment you experience at the time.

What makes temptations so destructive is that they never dissipate or go away completely. You may enjoy yielding to one and as soon as the indulgence is over, you are tempted again. Perhaps even more so. That is the dark side of temptation. Even those enticements that appear to be harmless or light-filled carry within them a seductive insatiability. That insatiability draws you away from yourself, thus your spirit, thus your faith and thus from God.

You find that when your heart is filled with love of God, little tempts you anymore. You are already full to brimming. There is nothing you need or want. There is no void—hunger or longing—except, perhaps, to be even more fully at one with God than you already are.

When you notice that you rarely must make tradeoffs or choose between the lesser of two evils, you may well have found your way more completely to God. And when you are with God, you are and have more than enough.

FULLNESS

Faith is the fullness of spirit within. It flows into your being with the effortlessness of a breeze on a summer afternoon. It graces your days with a subtle yet ceaseless joy. This fullness takes the place of other less enlightened aspects of your consciousness. As you transcend your inability to have faith, you make room for spirit.

Faith brings fullness to your life in ways that little else can. You are a vessel for that fullness. You have infinite capacity to imbibe the ecstasy and effervescence of faith. You also have the means to share your faith indelibly with others.

Once you become full of the love of God, you will find that the emptiness you felt and the hunger you experienced, as you were unsuccessfully attempting to fill yourself with anything but spirit, dissipates. You empty yourself of false sources of fullness and fill yourself with the only thing that can genuinely remain with you: God's love.

God's love is the one truly infinite and irreplaceable

aspect of your existence. All else is both finite and change-able. But the love of spirit—and your faith in its perpet-ual breath within you—leaves you eternally full.

If you are eternally full, you will no longer spend your days rushing around trying to assure the fullness of your existence in other ways. If you are eternally full, you will be confident that you will always be and have enough. If you can be and have enough, then there are no gaps to fill, no cracks in your vessel of being.

What causes the cracks in the first place: those open-ings where faith drains away and you are empty of spirit once again? You create a crack every time you adopt the desperate viewpoint that you must struggle and strain to make your way in the world. All of that struggle and strain drains your faith, not to mention your life force.

You create a crack in your spiritual vessel whenever you convince yourself that your life is no more than one quietly (or roaringly) desperate situation after another. Each one makes you even more desperate when the next one presents itself. Desperation does nothing to fill your vessel. It depletes it.

When we talk about desperation, we are not referring simply to the challenges you face. Everyone must deal with opposition and setbacks. How you approach them determines whether they make you desperate or more faith-full. If you believe that the worst will happen despite your best efforts, you will quickly grow desperate every time you encounter a difficulty. Your attitude becomes, "Oh, no, I'll never get through this one." And guess what? Often you do not.

You may encounter the same situation, but instead of feeling desperate, you feel full. That fullness energizes and inspires the way you face the challenge. You say, "This is going to be an exhilarating quest." And guess what? It is.

The fullness of spirit helps you maintain your faith regardless of what the material world presents to you. You have enough light, life and love to weather even the most extreme tempests. And when they are over and calm has returned, you realize that you are more full than ever.

Of course, life isn't always troubled. Your fullness of faith makes your contentment even more joyful. When you seize the moment with the self-confidence and charisma that accompany spirit, you create marvelous momentum behind your enthusiasm. How can things not be effortless, flow naturally and carry your faith toward your fullness, when you love life, living and letting go?

The fullness of faith helps you anticipate each day from the perspective of delight rather than dread. It creates a hope within, allowing you to be as innocent as a child and wise as a sage. It enables you to embrace each day with gusto—and not a little panache.

We come full circle, then, on our journey to fullness. As you describe and affirm the strength and stability of your faith, you experience a shift in how you approach the moments that punctuate your days. You realize that the traumas that used to bedevil you are less frequent— and have less impact when they do occur. In their place you are relishing extended periods of grace, or at least effortlessness and fulfillment.

What has changed is not the events in your life as much as your attitude toward them. You are given an opportunity for discovery and find that indeed you are on an even more courageous path than you ever thought possible. You hit a bump in the road and your faith cushions the impact. It serves as the shock absorber that it actually is.

That is fullness: in your life, in your heart, in your faith. Love fills you with more than you will ever need. And that love derives from your faith, which is waiting to be accessed and affirmed.

GRACE

Grace is the penetrating existence of spirit within you, guiding, comforting and leading you toward oneness with God. This oneness can be attained while you are in this body, in this lifetime. In fact, the reason you are in this body in this lifetime is to attain such a state of grace. You came here to do nothing but that.

States of grace enable you to acutely sense the presence of spirit. And that presence empowers you to see beyond the obvious, to harmonize with the larger patterns of the life force that surrounds you, and to be at one with the material and metaphysical worlds in which you reside. This at-oneness is possible not because you have dropped out of the world, but because you have embraced it wholly, joyfully and unreservedly.

When you are experiencing a state of grace, there are no boundaries between you and the larger flow of the forces of nature. You produce no resistance to the way spirit nurtures and nudges you. You feel so secure in your choices and the directions they carry you, you hesitate not at all.

Such states of grace are evidence of God's love. To experience a state of grace is to know fully what it is to be guided by the divine hand of spirit. To be in a state of grace is to trust more than ever before that you are so profoundly and completely infused with spirit, you cannot make a misstep. To breathe in the blessings of grace is to recognize your inherent divinity, to perceive that you may actually be far more spirit than flesh.

Grace is God's love showered down upon you, with its abundant devotion and peaceful reassurance. Grace does not descend like a thunderbolt, hurling itself at you from out of nowhere and causing you to recoil in awe or fear. Rather, grace subtly approaches you on the wings of divine knowing. You are blessed with grace because your soul longs for it—and because your goodness has earned it.

Does that make grace a reward for good deeds? Not at all. There is no quid pro quo for benevolence beyond the reward of knowing that you have acted selflessly and with open-heartedness. That in itself is recompense enough. But at times, often when you least expect it, God smiles down upon you. And those rays of love and joy overtake your consciousness, infusing it with an extraordinary contentment: serenity coupled with an absolute knowing that God is more completely with you than ever.

The conjoining of God's love with your spirit creates a state of grace. When you are in such a state, you feel both elevated above material reality and astutely, knowingly, gracefully integrated with it. Grace enables you to decide without being limited by doubts, to act with confidence that your purpose is at one with God's love, to create a transformed sense of your potential that far transcends how you defined yourself previously. Grace is the clear, crystalline presence of God in your life.

We could spend an entire volume describing the state of grace. But words alone provide only a pallid approximation of the actual experience. We fervently hope and fully expect that at many moments in your life, you will be blessed with the experience of grace. You are on the path, embracing your own spirituality and divinity more fully. And thus you will draw God's grace to you.

Grace can leave you as inexplicably and unpredictably as it arrives. You cannot hang onto it, or store it away to experience it at another time, or boast about it and expect it to endure. Welcome the arrival of grace the way you would a good friend, wise mentor or loving family member. Enjoy its presence in your life; revel in how much more fully you experience life because of it; but do not try to coax it to stay. The moment you attempt to grab hold of grace to assure its ongoing presence, you will cause it to vanish.

The awareness of who you are as a grace-full being enhances your faith immeasurably. After all, there is nothing like the full integration of spirit into your inner depths to give you an experience of the divine. And your experience of the divine in such a plausible, palpable way leads you to become far more comfortable with your faith.

To experience the unseen God as seen through the eyes of grace is to unfetter your faith. This leads you to the still waters of the heart, where your deepest oneness with God resides. It also leads to your capacity to be both spirit and flesh, divine and ordinary, enlightened and living fully in the here and now.

LIGHT

As a child of God, you have infinite capacity to embody love and light. As a child of God, you also have unlimited potential to evolve toward oneness with your source, which is God. As a child of God, you have the opportunity to release the bondage of your mortality and don the cloak of immortality, even as you remain in this body in this lifetime.

The promise of your current existence is that you will integrate light and love into your life so joyfully and passionately that you quite literally become nothing but light and love.

That is a breathtaking concept: to become nothing but light and love, despite your being bound in a mortal body. We are offering you not intimations of immortality, but the experience of it. Now, in this lifetime, at this moment in the history of planet Earth.

You have the capacity to become a being of light. Even though your physical body is composed of dense matter, it was designed to have enormous vibratory range. In other words, your physical body can become a vessel of light. You can, in this embodiment, transmogrify into light to such an extent that you are unseen in the physical world.

You are not in any way limited by your physical being. In fact, your body is only partially the dense mass you perceive it to be. Have you ever considered that your body might be an illusion, a construct firmly planted in material reality, that can actually take the form of a higher dimensional light body?

You are both physical and metaphysical. You are a collection of cells vibrating on the physical plane. You are also a vehicle of light, vibrating at a frequency that is so high, you are invisible to the naked eye.

Built into your metaphysical being is the possibility of transcending the boundaries of your earthly existence and accessing the infinite potential of your spiritual presence. When that occurs, the fences around your light environment fall away. You experience no need to assure your survival or to invest in your attachments. Your light being vibrates at a level closer to the Christ light than to that aspect of consciousness that defines your membership in the human family.

We see your light, even as you feel that you are living in the darkness, or semi-darkness. We recognize your commitment to spirit, even as you experience your own traumas and trepidations. We mirror for you the multifaceted measure of your existence, with its pleasures and profanities, transcendental opportunities and transformative tendencies.

And yet we relish your being far more than your becoming. We celebrate who you already are as an enlightened spirit in human form. We honor your commitment to God even as we recognize the chasm you must cross to deliver on that commitment. We love you for your shining inner light, which remains glowing and ever growing throughout the storms and dark tempests that your soul encounters.

If you take only one thing away from reading this volume, let it be this. You already are light and love. You have already stretched far beyond the material nature of your being. You already know what it means to be enlightened. You already are acting from your most humbly loving and selfless self.

We see this and rejoice. We also see that far from enjoying being enlightened, you believe that you are anything but. When you believe without question that you are a being of light, when you accept without ego your remarkable spiritual nature, when you find within a reservoir of gratitude that is never depleted, you embrace the fullness of your being.

And then the most marvelous miracle of all presents itself quietly at your feet. You see yourself as spirit, not just flesh; light and love, not just limitation and lethargy; formless, fathomless joy, not just sadness and suffering.

Allow yourself to believe that what we are telling you is not only possible, but has already been achieved by your soul. Then and only then can you release the stranglehold of your lower, unevolved self and walk instead into the light of the living and all-pervasive God, who is within you and synonymous with you.

Be brave. Be love. Be your most enlightened you.

BEHOLD

We complete this collection of messages—and this series of books—with a prayer. It came from us through Saint Benedict in the sixth century A.D. Gates discovered it not by accident at Westminster Abbey in London on the journey that enabled her to bring down these writings on faith. And she wrote it in her journal, not knowing that in the end we would lead her back to it just as she was completing this work.

The prayer of Saint Benedict asks this:

Give us the wisdom to perceive thee, diligence to seek thee, patience to wait for thee, eyes to behold thee, a heart to meditate on thee and a life to proclaim thee.

We bless you with it. We offer our assurances that if you make this prayer your own, it will be heard and answered. Whatever your choice, know that we surround you with our limitless love and spiritual sustenance. For we love you as God does.

Peace and peace and more peace be with you.

Amen.

Gates McKibbin never imagined that after spending twenty years as a management consultant specializing in strategic renewal, she would publish profound spiritual messages communicated from her deceased father, John McKibbin. For most of her adult life she had balanced a fulfilling professional career and a fascinating spiritual quest. Quite unexpectedly, her father, who visited her on the earth plane frequently after his death, began sending telepathic messages for her to write in her journal.

With Dad as her spiritual co-author, those original messages evolved into a seven-book series. The grace of direct contact enables Gates to converse with spirits as easily as she does with people. Her speeches and workshops generate a palpable sense of the presence of spirit, and her private consultations are redolent with insights from the other side.

Gates navigates adeptly through her roles as mystic, author, speaker and business consultant. She loves helping people discover their own unique path of spiritual transcendence. She also finds fulfillment in her work with companies facing turbulent change.

Born and raised in central Illinois, Gates now resides in San Francisco. She holds a Ph.D. from the University of Illinois and has received numerous academic awards, among them Phi Beta Kappa.

VISIT OUR WEBSITES

www.gatesmckibbin.com

www.lifelineslibrary.com

♦ Read excerpts from all seven books by Gates McKibbin

♦ Access the latest messages that Gates has received from the spirit world

♦ Talk with others about your own path to spirit

♦ Find out about how to order books and other products by Gates McKibbin

♦ Learn about Gates' upcoming public appearances

♦ Schedule a book signing event, workshop or speech by Gates McKibbin

LIFELINES LIBRARY ORDER FORM

FEATURING BOOKS BY GATES MCKIBBIN

Book Title	Quantity	Total Cost
The Light in the Living Room: Dad's Messages from the Other Side $9.95		
LoveLines: Notes on Loving and Being Loved $9.95		
A Course in Courage: Disarming the Darkness with Strength of Heart $9.95		
A Handbook on Hope: Fusing Optimism and Action $9.95		
The Life of the Soul: The Path of Spirit in Your Lifetimes $9.95		
Available Wisdom: Insights from Beyond the Third Dimension $9.95		
Forging Faith: Direct Experience of the Divine $9.95		
Complete set of seven books in the LifeLines Library $39.95		
Subtotal		
CA residents add 8.25% sales tax		
Postage and handling: $2/ book; $6/set		
Total enclosed		

Ship to:

Name_____

Street_____ Apt._____

City_____ State_____ Zip_____

Phone: _____ Fax_____

E-mail: _____

Mail your order to: McKibbin Publishing, Inc., P.O. Box 470091, San Francisco, CA 94147

Visit our Website at www.gatesmckibbin.com

Also available from **www.amazon.com**